MY LIFE MATTERS

Printed and bound in the United States of America

Editor: Casha Robinson, Seeds of Love Publishing

Content Editor: Je Tuan Lavyonne

Published By: Seeds of Love Publishing,

P.O. Box 722338,

Houston, TX 77272,

Business Phone: 832-323-3683.

Dedication

*This book is dedicated to every woman brave
enough to speak up!*

Acknowledgements

These are the many women that inspire ME to be a better ME!

Irene Patterson, Casha Robinson, Dawniel Winningham,
Dr. Natalie Francisco, Dee C. Marshall, Dr. Sonya Sloan,
Pastor Yolanda Carroll, Pastor Cassandra Scott,
Cynthia Sisto Wenz, Apostle Bernice White,
Minister Jackie Hill, Arlene Brown, Ava Graves,
Sylvia Jones, Traci Cooper, Kim Roxie

Contents

Introduction

Margaret Wheatley has been quoted to say, *"Be brave enough to start a conversation that matters."* For many years, I have noticed from our local to national news that reports story after story and number after number shocking disparities that happens in women's lives. These messages have been clear and consistent that women have become discouraged, disgusted, and frustrated. They have given up on looking for respectable jobs. They have given up on the judicial system. They have given up on their marriages. They have the fear of what's next after traumatic life experiences. They have even giving up on the church; because, they've found out their spiritual leaders are not God and have just as many issues as they do. I heard one woman share with me, "I am so sick and tired of being sick and tired."

What I've discovered is that there are a lot of broken women. They are secretly broken physically, spiritually, emotionally, and financially. They can't see past where they are and have given up hope on what's ahead. They have lost the zeal of experiencing what we've heard so often called "The American Dream". I mean from the best neighborhoods to the worst across America, every woman is experiencing the turbulence of trouble that is causing her to say, no I just give up. I quit. My life doesn't matter anymore.

With the current pop culture today, there is no sense of realness to address the issues that women are embarking on in this time. We are being portrayed as caddy women—arguing, fighting, back-biting, disloyal, forming cliques and expressing what's in-it-for-me. We are afraid to come forth and share the real truth of how we are feeling by wearing mask. We mistrust because of hurts. We are misinformed because of ignorance. We've been told you can't. You shouldn't do this or you shouldn't do that. I wouldn't if I were you. With all this before us, it is hard to seek out the right type of help. If we cannot be true to the person in the mirror, then how are we to be true to someone else?

What I found interesting in the Book of Ruth, there were two women who were faced with troubled times. There was a young woman by the name of Ruth, who was a princess. She was the great granddaughter of King Eglon of Moab. She was married to Mahlon, who later died, which made Ruth a young widow. There was Naomi, who was a woman of wisdom. Yet, Naomi allowed the cares of this world to cause her to become bitter and to lose hope on what's to come. Both of these women were faced with the same situations that were hopeless. They both had no husbands, no money and no means to take care of them. I don't know if you're aware of this, but in those days, widows had no standing in the community and were totally dependent upon the good-will of their families and friends for survival. It was the duty of the priests to look after widows and orphans, but there was no such provision in Moab; because, there was famine in the land. After examining their situation, they decided it was time to move on. They both decided to go to Bethlehem.

There is a practical purpose for the Book of Ruth, and we often miss this. You see, this book has something to say to all of us, if we are God's daughters. This is a book about redemption and revival. It is about friendship, healing, mentorship, and obedience. If we read all about it and know all about it and don't experience personal redemption and personal revival, well, we might as well have never read the Book of Ruth in the first place. You see, it's got to hit us personally. This is a personal journey that God is calling on you. Whether you are a mentor, mentee or just in preparation of mentoring others, it is time for you to go deeper. It is time for you to search deep on the inside of yourself and ask yourself: Why am I here? Why am I the way I am? Why do I keep going through these same vicious cycles of relationships that end in misunderstanding? Why do I always play the blame game? Why am I sitting on my gift of helping others? Why can I not get along with other women? All my friends are men? What? Are you kidding me, sis, all your friends are men?

In the pages that follow, you will read about women I mentor of all ages and experiences, who have shared with real and honest transparency about their struggles, hurts, pains, disappointments, and fears. All of life's influences have kept them from being the women they know they were created to be. You never know what a woman go through until you get to know her. I heard a saying once "know me before you label me". Each of these women shares their pasts, their present, and where they hope to be in the near future. With brave honesty and courage, each of us—and yes us, because I am included—share what's on our hearts to what we are feeling. In a simple declaration, we are sharing, *"My life Matters"*.

As I was praying about this book, I envisioned the scene of these women on a girl's weekend get-a-way retreat. Its dinner time and we start off in the kitchen. There is one cooking at the stove stirring in the pots; two cutting up vegetables; two using their very creative artistic gifts setting the dining table, two women sitting on barstools just watching, while two on their phones taking selfies, busy on social media, sharing some profound wisdom quotes; each of us participating in this conversation. We eventually move to the dining room area where we see the table is beautifully set for us. We are all at awe; it is breathe-taking!

I believe there is therapeutic value when women come together and share. It allows us the freedom, honesty of messiness, and the truth of longing for genuine authentic relationships that will eventually evolve to friendships. If you think about it, we are the gender that has been known for coming together and talking for hours. We always congregate around a good cooked meal. We share issues that manifested the mystery, the charm, and the strength. With those shared together, come fears and insecurities common to many women. The question raised here: who can I trust? Why would I want to share? Let along know what other women are battling—what I'm battling? Mentor, what is that? Is it a woman who for some morbid curiosity wants to know my business?

Oprah Winfrey has stated, "A mentor is someone who allows you to see the hope inside yourself. A mentor is someone who allows you to know that no matter how dark the night, in the morning, joy will come. A mentor is someone who allows you to see the higher part of yourself, when sometimes, it becomes hidden to your own view. I think mentors are important, and I don't think anybody makes it in the world without some form of mentorship."

Nobody makes it alone. Nobody has made it alone. And we are all mentors to people, even when we don't know it. We all need someone to listen to us from time to time and be real with us. I recognize that I serve as a spiritual mentor and/or sister-friend to many women. Anybody who makes it or anybody who achieves any level of success renders a testament to the world that accomplishments are obtainable; and you can be successful also. It is my prayer that you come along on this retreat with us, enter into the dining room, and have dinner with us and join in this girl-talk conversation. I pray that you will find these stories to be like footsteps: marking your own paths, recapping where you've been, shedding insight into your present, and revealing where it is you want to go, and that is your own Bethlehem—home. And so, here are the stories of your new friends.

Doves Love,

Cynthia A. Patterson

Chapter 1 - Let Go, Move On

*Sometimes the hardest lessons learned can be
the simplest if we listen.*

— Krystal

Krystal's Story

*Growing up without my father, longing and searching for
a father's love, was a huge struggle for me. My mother's
boyfriends became a father to me, but that only lasted for a
short period of time; because eventually, they would disappear.
After being sexually assaulted by a man I often intimated as my
favorite left my heart so cold, my level of worthiness was taken
from me. I made a promise to myself that I would never allow
someone that close to me hurt or harm me like that again. So,
I relocated after high school graduation to find myself in a city
where no one knew who I was. I eventually met a man, and we
had a child. This man made me feel safe, secure and loved.
Until love became so blind, I lost myself in the relationship; I
was lied to, cheated on, abused, and then ultimately, kicked out
of my home. My three week old baby and I had nowhere to live.
I was jailed; I had fights and arguments with different women.*

I was in a five year relationship of drama, lies and being manipulated. I could have had my own reality show -- UN-SCRIPTED! I longed for a family of my own. I wanted to experience a two parent home. I wanted my child to have a mother and a father, even if that meant me enduring all that pain. It was so hard for me to move on from him, because I believed our souls were tied. Soul Ties can be so strong when you love a person, especially if you share a child with that person.

A mother always puts her children first. A good mother protects her child. I felt like I would be hurting my daughter, if she didn't have her father around. I knew what I experienced growing up, not having my father around. My biggest fear was my child having to go through what I went through at a young age, but I refused to allow that cycle to continue.

One thing I was taught at a young age was how to pray. Prayer has always been my foundation when I needed to converse with God for His protection. I remember when my mother left me with my great grandmother, while she went away with a man. I remember getting off the bus, and two men chase me behind a city garbage can and began to rape me. I was still in elementary school, when this took place. I remember screaming and my great granny heard me. I remember opening my eyes to see my grandmother running water and making me get into the shower. All I could think about was being with my mother. I could hear my great grandmother saying a prayer as the water ran on my body. I had chills and cried so much that night. I can remember her telling me that nothing happened to me, that I just had a bad dream and not to ever mention my dream to anyone; and I didn't. That was one out of two times that I was sexual abused. At a young age, all I knew how to do was pray, to keep my mind clear from either harming myself or turning into a person that no one couldn't recognize. As I became an adult, God placed people in my life, even during the traumatic time in my five year relationship with my child's father. They would pray with me, talk me through, and give me advice on how to handle different situations.

Sometimes the hardest lessons learned can be the simplest, if we listen. I remember calling my mentor Cynthia and telling her that I needed God to change some things around in my life. I was in a season where I believed God was shifting me into another direction, but I had no clue of what that was. We would wake up every morning at 6:30 a.m. for prayer. I downloaded a bible app where I went through a 21-day process to breakthrough depression. I started journaling things I wanted God to do in my life, where I wanted God to take me, and the processes I was willing to take to be in position for God to bless me. I was so honest about the way I was feeling. These processes lead me to tell my mother about the sexual abuse. It allowed me to let go of my five year relationship. It gave me a sense of peace. It felt good to follow God. It felt amazing to see what God can do if you just obey and believe in His word.

I tell you right now I am free. I have a career, a college degree, and I have a wonderful man of valor in my life. We have a child together. I've never experienced this type of love. Even if my daughter doesn't have her biological father active in her life, she has such an amazing person who is there teaching her and showing her a father's love. He is a God fearing person. Everything I desired for my daughter and me, God has granted. Now I am clear that my purpose is to teach women that we fall, but we get back up. No matter what, if we pray and allow God to use us, He will bless us. I thank God for all He has done for me, because I'm able to tell my story and show that you can overcome anything.

Be Patient

I am so blessed by this story of Krystal. Five years is a long time. Here is the point— there are times your mentee will not get it at first. There will be times where she will continue to make the same mistakes over and over again, but remember it is for her to learn. It is for her to come into the knowledge of wanting more and to experience God for herself. You have to be patient and be willing for her to grow, and know the seeds of encouragement you have planted will eventually grow, and God will cause the increase in her life. You have to have a discerning heart to know when it is her season for change. And when that season comes, you have to be there to walk with her all the way to her blessing.

Your Ruth is Waiting

When Naomi discerned and finally accepted that Ruth was determined to go with her, she stopped urging her. Now in the previous two versus, Naomi's second daughter-in-law, Orpah could not discern the blessings ahead. Orpah made a decision to cancel out her blessing. Orpah was a woman full of unbelief and empty of wisdom. As a result, she made a mistake on making a now decision on a then experience. She was limiting her future to her past. She had more faith in her lack than she had in the promise. And when you meet a woman that does that, you have to understand she is limiting herself on what she could be based upon what she has been. And just like Orpah, she becomes preoccupied with problems and situations—when we should be looking at opportunities.

Read this closely and please understand. Your life matters. Your time matters and you have Ruth, eager and ready. You cannot keep trying to help Orpah; because she is not ready. You cannot keep reaching out to be her savior; only God is her Savior. She is in what we call the *"**Precontemplation** Stage of her change. Meaning, the **stage** at which there is no intention for her to change behavior in the foreseeable future. Many women in this stage are unaware or under aware of their problems"*.

11

(Cherry, 2014) This is something I had to learn the hard way. Thank God I have matured and able to discern. Now, I keep it moving and focus on what's ahead. Set a date reminder on your calendar in your phone to call her periodically. Like her Facebook, Twitter, and Instagram from time to time. You have to keep her in arms reach to let her know you are there. So when the time comes, she will be opened to return.

The most important thing that we could ever do is make the decision that no matter how many times we fall, we will always get back up. We must make the decision to keep doing what we know to do, and the results will come, if we make the decision to stay motivated and keep going! Ruth did not allow herself to be paralyzed by her lack of a husband. She understood God's promised provision and was willing to position herself for favor. She understood it would take an act of obedience, diligence and was able to receive the blessings of God. She understood that being in position for favor with God is predicated on her next decision. Her discernment let her know it was time to move on. She was able to discern when there was a season of change. It was time to let Go and Move on with her life. She told Naomi *"Don't urge me to leave you or to turn back from you. Where you go I will go, and where you stay I will stay. Your people will be my people and your God my God."*

Let it Go

For me the secret to a blessed life is a selective memory. Letting go of the past that has caused us the most pain or the most shame is hard. Wasting our lives with a false start of tomorrow will delay us, or we will never start at all. You were never born to fail. You were never born to live in turmoil. As we mature as a woman, we tend to have more stress, burdens, thoughts, decisions, fears, drama, and possibly less dreams. Or we have dreams, but they fall low on our priority list, because we feel our dreams aren't important, or we don't have faith that they can become a reality.

As a mentor, there are times when God is going to reveal to you that you are still holding on to circumstances of the past. These things are causing you to be stuck. We are unable to move forward in our lives, because we are holding on to what was, instead of what is to come. You have to understand that releasing and letting go is like spring cleaning—getting rid of the unwanted, old, damage, and dirt. This is the time to reflect on our lives and thoughts. Then gather and let go of the unwanted, dirt, damage, crap, negativity—you get the point? You can find your own creative way to release and let go. Maybe you run a mile for every release, maybe you can put a dollar in a jar every time the thought comes up, or maybe you journal your thoughts and feelings, allowing you to let go and never think or speak of those things again.

Sometimes we will be living in a difficult space. We have to quit looking at our situation and start anticipating our blessings. If you are having difficulties in a relationship, get past it. Don't be so preoccupied with your current situation that you don't see beyond it. As a mentor, you will have women in your life that may be in situations that is too hard to let go. It may be hard for them to move forward. Realize there is a process and there are times when patience is the essence to who you are as a mentor. You cannot allow your beliefs are situations to get in the way of another woman's deliverance because of what you had to go through. I learned this from my mentee, Krystal.

If you are a mentor or think you are called to mentor others, you will not succeed if you are still holding onto some things. You can't do that if you have what I call "your stuff" blocking you from seeing. "Your stuff" are things like unforgiveness, bitterness, anger, jealously, and every other offense that comes with "your stuff" getting in the way. Get "your stuff" out of the way and allow God to do what He does best. This is what life is about, right? We go through so many stages in life that require shifts in our thoughts, actions, and goals. Tell me, are you at a point to let go and move on? Are you looking to let go of a thought or a past experience? Is it time to spruce up your dreams and goals? It's never too late to make changes in your life, so take some time to reflect and decide if there is anything in your life or in your mind that you need to let go of and move forward.

Chapter 2 - No U-Turns

*It is up to us to recognize the good that is
'always in our suffering*

— Veronica

Veronica's Story

*T*urning back is so easy. It is the norm. It is what we do when
going the other way seems too difficult. Spiritually, I can
relate to this very well. When I first went off to college, I felt
that my relationship with God was so strong that nothing could
steer me in the wrong direction; but in reality, I really did not
know who I was at that point. So without knowing yourself
in and out— your strengths and weaknesses—you can't even
know what you are vulnerable to. You don't know what to stay
away from, because you don't know who you are! Just think
about it.

So while being in this confused state about myself, I was
very vulnerable, especially when it came to guys and falling
in love. I was in a broken relationship for over three years,
but in the end, it had made me so much stronger. My mentor
Minister P. would say to me, "Your sense of self-worth comes
from knowing that you are strong, powerful and capable to do

17

anything the next person can!" I know that my sense of self-worth was strengthened after this relationship. I felt that God was with me—truly with me—each step of the way and never left my side.

So now when I face something, I don't just think I am not alone, I know that I am not alone. That is why I value myself more, because the way that God sees us, we don't even recognize one tenth of that value within ourselves. As I read my books and spend time in prayer more and more, I sense the power that is within me to do great things. I sense peace and purpose beyond me. I am starting to realize more and more that the things I am searching for are already here. I already have them within me. If I want love, I have an abundance of love from God and an overwhelming love for me. If I want peace, I can pray and it will be there. It is already there in the midst; we just do not fully recognize it.

I think so much we turn our senses onto the negative like anger, sadness, jealousy, but the loving qualities are always within us. It just depends on how we decide to feed into our energy. That is why I am so big on the company I keep. I can't have people around me that always have something bad to say about their lives. Don't get me wrong, some people are struggling; but it is up to us to recognize the good that is always in our suffering as well. There is always some good, and I like to

be around others that recognize that so that we won't be feed-
ing into negative energy.

One day I decided to make a list of things that I enjoy doing
the most and will bring me the most peace and satisfaction.
Then on the other side of the list, I wrote what stops me from
doing them. After reading the list I discovered, it can help you
evaluate why you do some of the things you do. I've learned
from Minister P. that sometimes we don't even know why we
are doing things; we just get so caught up in doing them that
we continue, but we forget what makes us the most joyful. This
goes back to why people make U-turns. It is because we do
not recognize that the U-turn will not bring us the most peace.
It will, in fact, do just the opposite. When you recognize this
and are fully aware of what brings you those peaceful, happy
moments, you will not even want to U-turn. That is the place I
got to in my life; I was so happy until there was no way I would
think of turning back again!

Position for Purpose

Veronica has made a precise valid point. We have to get rid
of the pessimism, because if we keep looking over our lives
and continue to focus on the negativity that happened in our
lives, all we seemed to see are things that cause us to become
bitter, angry or resentful. We must do whatever we have to do

to get out of the snare and trap of the enemy. Warning! Warning! Let me shout it loud, and let me shout it clear. Do not allow anything that anyone does to you make you bitter, angry, or resentful, because they will cancel out your blessings. Ephesians 1:11 *"In Him also we have obtained an inheritance, being predestined according to the purpose of Him who works all things according to the counsel of His will."*

When you decide to move forward, expect some highs and lows. Positioning for purpose is predicated on your next decision. Now the trip for Ruth and Naomi from Moab to Bethlehem would have taken between seven to ten days. It would have required them to cross the Jordan River and climb the 2000 plus feet in elevation to reach Bethlehem. It would have been easy for them to stop short of the city. It would have been easy for them to make a U-turn, but they continued until they were where they were supposed to be!

Or it could have been a situation where Naomi was physically tired, mentally exhausted and just followed the lead of Ruth. Naomi's attitude could have been like, "girl whatever". "I'm good." "You go ahead." That would have been a tragedy! Ruth had never traveled that way before; she was from Moab. Ruth was not familiar with the roads traveling to Bethlehem. Ruth could have been impatient and said, "Naomi, I will see you in Bethlehem. I heard going east would be quicker." Not understanding that east is the wilderness.

Doesn't this sound familiar? How many times have you, Veronica and I been impatient and wanted to go in another direction. Whether it is us or others, places or things that influences our decision making, as a mentor, it is very important that you are decisive in your decision making. It is very important that you help your mentee stay focused on the goals that were established for her. It is also important that you help her process the knowledge she have already received. Often, we assume all women respond the same way in receiving information, finding the truth, and making life changes.

Tears Are Okay

I would often tell Veronica, watch your thoughts; they become words. Watch your words; they become actions. Watch your actions; they become habits. Watch your habits; they become character. Watch your character; it becomes your destiny. As a mentor, you have to make sure you are providing primary care to your mentee. We are relationally focused and desirous of understanding and support. Emotional processing proceeds decision making. It is up to us to make sure that our mentees are emotionally stable. Understand that she cannot think about her options, about what she ought to do until she has first worked through her feelings. We often cry, but seldom apologize for it. Unlike men, they tend to put their feelings on hold, until they have had a chance to get their thoughts on the table. They put their thoughts before feelings. Men are afraid they will break down emotionally during counseling. When men do cry, they usually apologize.

In Ruth 1:9-10 Naomi and her girls cried together, *"May the Lord bless you with the security of another marriage."* *Then she kissed them good-bye, and they all broke down and wept. "No," they said. "We want to go with you to your people."* This clearly lets us know that we need freedom to emotionally process our feelings to cry. We need someone to help us think through our options. A woman needs to make a well thought out decision regarding her next step to bring logical thought into this process. However, the order of this process is often ignored. If the truth be told, we cannot easily think about the options, until we have worked through our feelings.

Help Your Mentee Process Knowledge

Working through her feelings is very important. Another critical area of understanding is how your mentees think and process knowledge. Your role in her life is to be a sounding board to work things through and to connect the dots for solutions. Often times we make the mistake and assume all women respond the same to receiving information, finding truth, and making life changes. But this is not the case. Each of your mentees process learned information differently. So you can't assume she will get it the first time. Therefore, you must schedule some face-time with your mentee. I call these moments together "We-time". "We-time" is a personal one-on-one time for you to catch up and share. It is a time for your mentee to discuss with you her hopes and dreams. Most of us have strong cognitive abilities—how we process the knowledge we receive. Some of us are *Silence Knowledge*, where we do not have the ability to speak for ourselves. We accept any external authority blindly. We are mindless and voiceless. *Received Knowledge* is where women cannot see themselves as coming up with knowledge on their own. They listen to the voices of others. *Subjective Knowledge* is when these women reject outside advice. They only listen to their inner voice. They become their own authority. No guidance. No mentor. This as a result is destructive behavior. *Constructed knowledge* is when these women are creators of knowledge. They are able to integrate emotion and mind. She is a whole person. She has a passion and purpose for learning. She relates to others very well, empathizes and is sensitive to the inner being of others.

The differences that are reflected above are so profound. I am so glad Veronica and me were delivered. Through our breakthroughs, we were able to receive redemption through God's love. If you do not receive the strong support and encouragement, you will be tempted to make a U-turn. It's like walking on the treadmill—you're moving, but you are not going anywhere. No growth at all! Please remember, mentor, although there are some true generalities about the women you mentor, they all do not process life alike. Once you identify the differences, you can be more effective in mentoring according to their way of processing their life.

Don't Get Sidetracked

I have come to understand this walk is not easy. The journey gets complicated sometimes. There are ups and downs you have to experience, and it is the middle of our journey where we tend to make the decision to give up. I want to encourage you, because God is Alpha and Omega; He is the Beginning and the End. You must have the diligence to stay focused on the in between. Satan, who is effective at distracting you from God's best, wants you to continue to wallow in your pity parties. He wants to sidetrack you from making a lasting investment of hanging in there. We allow some things to consequently get in the way and delay our positioning.

We are born to live our lives to the fullest. We are going somewhere. We have goals and purposes, and we need some sort of road map to reach these goals. When we get up in the mornings, we make our plans for the day. We set objectives for the week. We have confidence that our job will generate the income, our health will prevail, and we can achieve the goal of living comfortably. We are singing the song by Jill Scott, "Living My Life Like its Golden".

But sometimes things go wrong. Our course gets rerouted. Something happens, and our plans don't always work out. Economic downturns jeopardize our jobs. Relationships change. Marriages may fail. We experience losses, and as a result, we have to change our plans and alter our goals. The journey changes; we are tempted to make a U-turn. When we decide to make a U-turn, we become frustrated. We experience anxiety, or we wonder if our direction will even get us to the destination.

Satan knows he can't do anything about our destiny, because it has been predestined. Hereafter, what he does is try to get down in our circumstance and throw us some reasons to want to quit. As a mentor, you have to help your mentee under-stand that God's purpose cannot be reversed, no matter what the enemy brings her way. She has to learn the art of shaking some junk off. She is heartbroken. She has been stabbed in the back. Or people are gossiping about her. Nonetheless, she cannot get caught up in the drama, because these are called destiny distracters. They will destroy her ability to make good godly decisions.

As her mentor, you have to beware and discern the times in her life—I talked about this in chapter one—or you will get frustrated and make a U-turn from helping her. You will have a judgmental spirit, and she will shut down on you and isolate herself from you. She won't answer your text, calls or emails. Unsatisfied and unfulfilled, you both sink deep into the quicksand of: "No, I can't do it"; "I don't think this is the season"; "She doesn't even listen to me"; "I've wasted all this time"; "That's why I don't deal with women. They are too caddying." Tell yourself right now, "NO is not an option". "I will not make a U-Turn". "I am going all the way to fulfill the purpose of God".

Chapter 3 - No Longer My Way

Whenever I am outside of God's will… I am heading
for destruction.

— Quin

Quin's Story

I had a recent situation where I found myself living life according to my own rules and standards and not by the word of God. I did not think that I was doing anything that could cause direct harm to my life, but I was wrong. I was wrong by not realizing that whenever I am outside of God's will that I am heading for destruction. In fact, I was delaying my spiritual growth and sabotaging my relationship with God.

I was in the prime of my career, and God was blessing me with a lot of opportunities to excel in my profession. I had recently received a promotion, making me the youngest manager within the company. Life was great. I started to spend most of my time at the office; in fact, I was typically the first one in and last one out of the office. However, with each opportunity for career elevation, I started to believe that I was responsible for driving my success. My ego started to get out of control, and

I began to believe that I was in total control of my life. I felt like I was calling the shots and ultimately deciding my destiny. I thought that I was in control of my career. When in reality, being out of my relationship with God, I was out of control.

I worked hard to keep my career a top priority, and everything else took a backseat to work, including my relationship with God. I thought that the more success I received in my profession, the more control I would have over my life. I gravitated towards believing that I was in control, and this allowed me to focus on my abilities, instead of God. Secretly, I was trying to create a lifestyle different from the one that I was nurtured in because of my own internal insecurities. I grew up being very critical of myself. I was trained to be extremely independent, and I pushed myself hard. While growing up my family, I endured a lot of financial hardships, and it was very important for me to make sure I did not live my adult life with the same financial challenges.

I knew I was out of God's will, when I was no longer bothered, when I sinned, and I could go into the office on Sunday mornings, instead of going to church. I could go days without talking to God, and I was not including God in my life decisions. My prayer life no longer existed. I continued to focus on work and neglected my relationship with God. Eventually, I was laid off. The fact that I no longer had a salary scared me, because I have always been responsible for taking care of myself. I took a lot of pride in my ability to support myself. I felt so alone and ashamed of my situation. I immediately began to think that losing my job was a result of my disobedience to God. My initial thoughts were God was dealing with me, because I had not been a good steward over what was entrusted to me. I knew that the way I was living did not glorify God. I did not know what would happen next, but I knew I needed to repent.

I found myself unemployed and devastated, but I knew if I could get in the presence of God, I would feel better about my circumstances. My church happened to be having a revival, and it was perfect timing for me, because I needed to reconnect with God. I went to church and spent the service praying that God would forgive me. It was the end of service, when I happened to see my mentor, Cynthia; and thank God, she has the gift of discernment, because I did not have to tell her that something was wrong with me. In fact, she knew before I opened my mouth. I was excited to see her, because I needed to discuss my situation. I began to tell her all about how I had been skipping church, as well as tithing. I was hurting so bad, because I knew my lifestyle was a disgrace to God. She shared with me that I had repented, and I needed to move forward, because God still loved me. However, I still felt doubtful that God could still love me after the way I had been behaving.

Fast forwarding the conversation, I did not tell Cynthia I was unemployed. Not because I was ashamed to share, but because I had too many other issues I wanted to share. During our conversation, another church member stopped by to say hello to Cynthia, and she introduced us and said to the other lady, "This is Quin. Remember I was telling you about her." Immediately the lady said, "Quin, I am looking a Corporate Recruiter for an Oil and Gas Company," I could not believe it, but my mentor was right. God still loved me. I began to tell Cynthia that I had lost my job the week prior, and I could not believe that God was still working on my behalf. To sum up the story, I took a position with that company in less than two weeks. I could not believe that God was willing to give me another opportunity so quickly. I made a decision to accept God's will when Cynthia shared with me that God was sovereign, and God had been in control of my life all along. She told me that my mistakes did not change God's love for me. In fact, God orchestrated my steps so I would see my mentor at church, and she would introduce me to someone that could help get me a job.

It was at that moment that I realized I controlled nothing, and God controlled everything. If God chooses to bless me with a job, great; but if not, I will still be taken care of, because God ultimately decides what will happen. I realized God was my provider, not my job. God's love for me still blows my mind, because He was faithful to me when I was unfaithful. God could have withheld the blessing from me; but instead, God chose to give me another chance. God gets all the Glory, and I can't get any credit for this one. It was all God. My pastor often says, "Everything we need is in God", and I really did not understand that until now. I am so grateful that God gave me the opportunity to witness something so amazing. I thought that I lost, when I lost my job; but, it was a gain. It was an opportunity to restore my relationship with God and to witness God's love for me. I got a job that God created especially for me. How can I not give him glory?

Positioning for Favor

It is time for you to wake up. God is positioning you for favor. The blessing is on the way. You have to be determined that "no is not an option; you are going all the way". Unfortunately, some of us can't say this and really mean it, because you have allowed Satan to distract you by the cares of this world. There comes a time when we become impatient, because we don't see anything happening. As a result, we tend to withdraw prematurely from a helping situation, because you are not seeing an immediate payoff for your efforts. That causes you to want to give up and throw in the towel. Why? It's important not to become overwhelmed by what's ahead of us and lose the hope and motivation to keep on moving? The bible says, *"Therefore also now, says the Lord, turn and keep on coming to Me with all your heart, with fasting, with weeping, and with mourning [until every hindrance is removed and the broken fellowship is restored]." ~ Joel 2:12 (Amplified Bible)*

God is saying you have to keep on coming, keep on fasting until every hindrance is removed, and the broken fellowship is restored. You should not allow anything, or anyone, to change your expression of confidence towards God. What can the enemy do to stop you? Nothing! Quin is one of the boldest and most confident women I have ever met. I appreciate her so much because of her drive. Just like many of us, she too got lost in the process.

Be in Tuned with your Mentee

It is very important that you are awake. When I say awake, I mean being in tuned with your mentees; because, they need to know God. They need to know the joy of forgiveness and a relationship with the Good Shepherd! It is my passion as a mentor to make sure everyone I come in contact will experience the resurrection power in their lives. Only a relationship with God can complete what a woman needs for health and wholeness. In my book "It Had to Happen" I use the woman with the issue of blood to illustrate what this look like. Jesus said in Mark 5:34, *"Daughter, you took a risk of faith, and now you're healed and whole. Live well, live blessed! Be healed of your plague."(Message Bible).*

I believe Ruth's commitment to Naomi went even further: *And your God, [will be] my God.* This was more than a change of address. Ruth was willing to forsake the Moabite gods she grew up with and embrace the God of Israel. She was deciding to follow the LORD. This Gentile woman, once far from God, had drawn near to Him. Likewise, this was an encouragement for Quin and me to grasp from one another, as well as understand that our current situation isn't the destination, but a chance to alter the course to get there.

Chapter 4 - Seeing Beyond Myself

No one is perfect, and with consistent healthy communication regarding feelings and thoughts, it is possible to not have to deal with disappointments.

—Pernilla

Pernilla's Story

I have high expectations for myself; so as a result, I naturally placed those same expectations on others. As an immature young girl growing up, I believed that my thoughts were pretty rational and practical; so, seeing things my way was pretty much the best way. However, I would never place expectations on others without considering the alternative. I would look at all aspects and consider the various outcomes, and I would usually arrive back at my expectations being priority and making the most sense. I had to learn that putting specific expectations on others is not always a fair thing to do. I have always expected others to honor their words and commitment. There have been several occasions where I felt let down, because I didn't feel like my mentor made my situation a priority. She dropped the ball on several occasions, by not attending several milestones that had taken place in my life. After two no shows, I then categorized my thoughts on where she should be in my life; however, I still invited her to major celebrations and victories. After missing the third event, I was still shocked and surprised, but not as bothered as the previous two occasions. Following this event, I knew I had to talk with her to have this difficult conversation. As a growing adult, I understand that you can't expect others do as you do. Everyone is different, and at times that can seem a bit unfair. Hence, I have learned to be flexible with my expectations and needs of others.

I have grown to think this way, because as a kid my parents gave me their undivided attention and support whole hearted-ly. In addition, I also had teachers in my life who talked with me about having goals, boundaries, and expectations for your-self and others. I was one spoiled kid as some would say, but I deserved it. I behaved well. I made all A's in school and served as a role model for my peers. Because of that, it was rare that people would not honor their commitments to me. I am grate-ful for parent and teachers who served as mentors, because together they assisted me in ensuring that I was grounded with morals and standards.

Our ability to relate to others and the importance we give to relationships are deeply intertwined, because growth and longevity is established through likes, differences, and a desire to be an intricate part of a person's journey. It also helps me to know when I've let someone down based on the expectations that I know the other person has for me, if they share their feelings with me or if their behavior is different around me. In addition, sometimes I know when I've let someone down based on me putting myself in their shoes. Whereas, other times I may not know; therefore, I need to be informed. Furthermore, I know when I have been let down, because I once felt great about the situation or person, and yet I find myself in conflict with the fact that due to an event that has taken place, I now feel skeptical or not as trusting as I normally would. However, it doesn't hinder me from moving forward or addressing any concerns or desires that I wish to come to past.

As I have matured, I try to control my actions. I realize that I am not in control of everything, but I know that I can control me and not others. If I stopped trying to control me, then I would probably be vulnerable and others would control me. Ultimately, God is in total control of me and all things. I have learned this through the relationship with my spiritual mentor, who has been a part of my walk for the last six years. I can honestly say that she has assisted me as a coach and big sister.

During the earlier stages of Cynthia getting to know me as a mentee, she recommended various books to help guide me through my spiritual walk. I am so glad that she took the time out to talk to me whenever I called. She also called to check on me periodically. I could count on her to be there for me! Our relationship is one of a sister to sister. Although there have been some disappointing times, I can say that the good definitely outweighs the few bad. Today, I think about how instrumental she has been in my life, and I wouldn't have it any other way. I will always have her in my life because of the sacrifices and the time she has dedicated to my life. I never asked her to be my mentor. She just landed in my life, and I'm grateful that God sent my personal Naomi.

God has a different life script that he has written for each of us. Your situation or obstacles that you have endured may not be the same as mine. However, I do know that we all face disappointing times, where we feel like we are not vital to the livelihood of the people that we believe matter most. While we may feel this way, it is important to know that no one is perfect. With consistent healthy communication regarding feelings and thoughts, it is possible to not have to deal with disappointments. While my mentor let me down more than a few times, I have forgiven her. I no longer allow the things in the past to discourage me from having an awesome relationship with her. In fact, if you have been in a similar situation, I encourage you to do the same; it's easier and the best way and most importantly God's way.

See Beyond Yourself

What a sad commentary! As a mentor, we have to be very careful with this, because we will experience burnout and won't be good to anyone. We have to see beyond ourselves and know there are expectations that others expect of us, and we must do our very best towards others in order to avoid any disappointments. Lack of support will potentially rupture a relationship, and if we are not discerning, it will cause us to cancel the very plans that God has for us and our mentee. This was such a revelation for me with my relationship with Pernilla.

Confront the Challenging Issues

Naomi and Ruth's relationship is one to be admired. In looking geographically the journey they had to take to Bethlehem, I would imagine there were some tough days. I would imagine some sacrifices they both had to make in making sure each other were emotionally good. I would think as the elder woman, Naomi was intentional in seeing after Ruth. They walked together during their journey through the sunshine days and rainy days. As a mentor, you have to realize there will be times God will allow your relationship to be tested with someone to whom you are called. You have to discern when that time comes and confront the challenging issues. Sometimes there are seasons where the two of you are required to grow. There are some tough decisions you have to make. There are some sacrifices you have to make. Yet during those tough times, during those sacrifices, during those unpleasant decisions, a mentor must communicate with their mentee. Since those are the very times you can jeopardize your relationship with your mentee. Trust me; I learned that the hard way, and it almost cost a very precious relationship.

It was at a time when my personal life and ministry life increased. The windows of heaven were opened, and God allowed me the opportunity to minister to more women. At the same time, God blessed me to be a first time Grandmother. God was doing amazing things in all my mentees life. It was a time of fruitfulness. It was a time of blessings. In the midst of all, I had become Martha, and I realized I had Super Woman Disorder (SWD). Yes, I had the SWD, where I became addicted to "trying to be all things to everyone". Underneath all the smiles, I was running on "empty" and was no good to anybody, not even myself. It was a time where I was so overwhelmed with responsibilities, and I had experienced the "B" word "Burnout". I have always said you have to do "life" with your mentee. With that being said, it is unrealistic when there are seasons as in *Ecclesiastes 3:1 "To everything there is a season, and a time to every purpose under the heaven"* where boundaries have to be established and clear communications of understanding are critical. I must admit; I did miss a few events

Pernilla had in her personal and ministry life. Foremost, one of her love language is Quality time, and attending her events is very important to her. Since I did not communicate what was going on in my life, it appeared that I no longer cared or had any interest.

God is in Control

I praise God for my relationship with Pernilla, because it allowed me to see that God is in control, if you are divinely connected with someone God has assigned you. I would imagine Naomi and Ruth journey was one that was very difficult. Plus on their way, there were situations and circumstances that caused them to either give up or keep going. I am so excited they decided to keep going. Moreover, in that perseverance to move forward, God was able to bless them far beyond what they could ever imagine. Likewise, Pernilla and I could not have done this on our own. It was nobody but God himself that revealed to us what He was doing in both of us. Most importantly, it was through this season in our relationship that God matured us to understand that our life matters, by fulfilling His purpose and seeing beyond ourselves.

Chapter 5 - I Shall Not Be Moved

I live my life and make decisions based on how God will judge me, not man.

—Tosha

Tosha's Story

I have to admit; it has not always been easy for me to trust people. I have always had the belief that people are only out to benefit themselves and have no genuine interest in the cares and concerns of others. People cater to their own needs and desires with little to no regard for how their actions affect others. I have lived my life in an extremely self-centered way, thinking that people are out to make my life miserable and to do me emotional harm. In reality, people probably care very little whether I am the most miserable or the happiest person on the face of the earth. I do not say this to sound cynical or to suggest that I am unloved. I say this to express that we can be excessively focused with own lives that we believe others are just as focused and concerned with our lives.

My biggest fear is being emotionally hurt and vulnerable. In order to avoid facing my fears, I opted to get into relation-

ships where I felt that I could control the dynamics. If I could control the person, as well as myself, then there was no way that I could get hurt. I lived by the proverb, "Get the person before they get you!" I would purposely sabotage my romantic relationships by behaving in a way that would create emotional distance between the men and me. I would force them into wanting to get out of the relationship. How is that getting them before they get me, if I put them in the position of ending the relationship? Strange as it may sound, that was power to me. I created the situation, not them. I forced their hands; they didn't force mine. In reality, I really was powerless, because I often found myself the one emotionally hurt in the end. I guess one can say that I was an emotional masochist. For me not to want to be hurt, I continued to welcome emotional pain. On some level, I believe I enjoyed the pain. I strived on feeling like the victim once the men left. I felt that I was incapable of being loved, but in hindsight, I was scared of loving and being loved. Being emotionally close to a man meant being "opened" and vulnerable, something that I refused to be. Courage is facing your fears, no matter the outcome and no matter the opposition.

I also believe it is human nature for everyone to have some fears. Just because one is a Christian does not exempt them from experiencing fears. Job, who described as perfect and upright (Job 1:1), was not without fears and apprehensions

(Job 3:25). The problem comes when we become paralyzed and controlled by our fears. Fear can only be conquered through faith in God. When we truly surrender our will and our lives to our Creator, fear no longer takes precedence.

When I suffered two debilitating episodes with anxiety and depression, my inability to overcome fear and anxiety in my life became markedly obvious. In 2002, after ending a tumultuous two year relationship, I found myself in the pits of darkness. I lost my ability to eat, sleep, and function daily. From nowhere, I begin having panic attacks. There were times when I contemplated suicide, not because the relationship was over, but because of what depression did to my mind. The overwhelming feelings of hopelessness, self-loathing, and loneliness can be extremely destructive. While the relationship was unhealthy, it was one that had made me comfortable and one where I thought I was truly in love. The toll of the break-up was too much on my psyche. At the time, I really did not understand the connection between my condition and the ending of the relationship. Now, I know that it wasn't the demise of the relationship that sent me to abyss of despair, but my need for control of myself and others. I spent two years unable to dominate the course of my relationship. I was so fearful of being cheated on, mistreated and abandoned that I created circumstances that drove my significant other away. My fear of being alone resulted in me being alone. This time alone was not by *happenstance, but by the will of God. God needed to put me in a position of dependence on Him. My issues of control needed to be addressed, and God desperately wanted me to relinquish control and turn my life completely over to Him.*

My second bout of depression and anxiety occurred in 2013. Once again, I allowed my inability to control circumstances around me send me to an anxiety ridden state. This episode left me fearful of driving, physically and mentally emaciated due to lack of sleep and food for more than three months. In addition, I was unable to function on my own and had to live with my mother and aunt during the duration. For someone as independent as I, this was devastating and embarrassing to say the least. Once again, God put me in a position of de-pendence on Him. The only explanation for me having sur-vived this ordeal was solely by the grace and love of God. God knows my weaknesses and my strongholds. As He did 11 years prior, God allowed me to be put in solitude in order to seek and rely on Him. God showed me that as long as I continue to seek my own understanding and go my own way, this "thorn" of anxiety and depression will continue to haunt me.

A fundamental truth that I credit Cynthia for instilling in me is the idea of being delivered from people. She always stressed the importance of "not allowing others to dictate your life and the decisions you make. We are here to please God, and not man. Everyone will not always agree or understand what God has ordained or commissioned someone to do, but it is our responsibility to do what God has called for us to do, in spite of others' opinions".

As I look back over the years, I am amazed that I still have my sensibilities. I read so many stories where mental illness had dominated a person's life, that suicide and confinement to an institution is the out. God gave me permission to take control over one thing in my life, and that is my depression and anxiety, and not allow it to control me. While I incurred moments of despair, they were just that, moments. After the episodes...life resumed; a life...where I was dependent and trusting in God.

Now I give myself permission to live and to make mistakes. I do not concern myself with what others think. I live my life and make decisions based on how God will judge me, not man. I have decided to change those things that I can change and control and accept those things that I cannot. I refuse to put self-imposed pressures on myself. My new philosophy is, "It is what it is."

Permission to Live

That is it—five key words: "give yourself permission to live". As a mentor, your purpose is to draw findings from

many of the arenas that impact a women's life, from intention-
ally identify the unique characteristics, behaviors, and needs of
your mentee, to the greater purpose of providing the care she
needs. As women, we are life-bearers, nurturers. Relationship
is the primary concern for us. I believe Naomi realized that
with Ruth. She realized Ruth needed her and allowed her to
travel the journey with her to Bethlehem. Together, they were
able to stand and not be moved.

Tosha is a woman—I believe has pushed through to see her
life change—, and with all the wherewithal, has overcome
great obstacles. No matter what the difficulty, she has been
able to find her way back to be responsive to God, enabling
Him to bend and shape her for His purposes and to prepare
her for His work. I have known Tosha for 15 years. I remember moments when Tosha would cry out to God, that's when I
knew He had His hands on her. She still surrenders and follows
God's lead and yields to His will. It was a long journey, but to
see where she is today… Wow!

Respond With Faith and Not Fear

Are you struggling through a situation today and are grasp-
ing for answers? How should you respond? I would suggest
that you respond with faith and not fear, knowing the promises
of God and His right hand will hold you through any situation.

I would imagine the fear that Ruth and Naomi may have felt as they got closer to their destination. I would imagine the long dark nights. They only had each other to depend on— two women walking a long journey with no one to depend on. During a time when it seemed as if all hope was gone. Even at a time when it felt that life dealt them a bitter blow, they were able to adjust, not only to maneuver through the journey, but to experience triumph on their arrival to Bethlehem.

People Pleasing Addict

As a mentor, I have made a decision not to allow the enemy to dupe the women I mentor. He gets very upset with me, because I refused to allow my girls to go through a spiritual episode of PUNK'D! Meaning he is trying to victimize them with tricks and lies. I am constantly in prayer and intercession on behalf of my mentees against spiritual warfare. See Satan has a way to tell you about your self-worth. Tell you that you are nothing. You are not pretty enough. You will not amount to anything. With all of these false accusations from the enemy, you have now become a People Pleasing Addict (PPA); but, you are to ignore those lies and instead believe what God says about you.

Chapter 6 - Knowing your Personal Truth

When God shines a light through you, there is nothing you
can do to hide it; no matter how hard you try.

— April

April's Story

*F*rom adolescence to adult hood, I honestly could not understand women. They were friendly one moment, then
attacking you behind your back in the next, all with a smile
on their face—when nothing about you had changed. In my
mind, if I wasn't rude or disrespectful towards them, it didn't
justify their actions toward me. So, I began to respond to them
just as ugly as they were to me, not realizing that I was taking
on their ugliness. It was a transfer of spirit. Naturally, I'm a
really friendly, considerate person; so acting this way, became
harder than my comfort level would allow. So, I started doing
things different in an effort to make things better. I started dull-
ing myself down, so others wouldn't feel like I was a threat. I
mean, if my hair is up and I wear less make up, maybe I won't
get as much attention. Right? Wrong!

Dealing with the insecurities of others can make you question yourself, if you are not equipped to understand that the actions of others has very little to do with you. Ruth could've easily been distracted by what others thought of her, but instead she focused on instruction. She was obedient to what she was being told. I learned that when God shines a light through you, there is nothing you can do to hide it; no matter how hard you try, even if you're the dummy young woman at the back of the field minding your own business. It's amazing how we can be surrounded by individuals that shield us from developing and knowing our own truth in an effort to continue to live their lie, or to make them comfortable.

I was so focused on the comfort level of individuals, that didn't know who they were, that I'd started losing the most important part of me, my personality. I was becoming someone that I not only recognized, but didn't like. I went from one extreme to another. I'd changed my mind, but had no concept of how to proceed with the process. My intentions were scattered in a targeted area. Until I was mentored, I recognized within myself that there was a process; but, I didn't know what it was or how to start. Not to mention, the distrust in women I'd developed in church and out. Eventually, I had to ask myself a very important question that most innate nurturers often shy away from. Why is the opinion and comfort of others more important to me than my own? I'd argue with myself back and forth, but realistically no matter how well we talk ourselves into great decisions, it is our actions that testify the truth that we believe in. At our most human level, our truths can very well betray us all why trying to prove us.

I had to be honest with myself and accept that I had given more of my attention away in an effort to seem better. Nonetheless, in order to actually become better, I would have to shift my focus to me and that I owed no one an apology for it. Often there are times manipulation can come about—as we are developing our truths and living in it—as an attempt to sabotage our development.

I've since learned that I was stronger than I thought; besides, it was that strength that people had recognized in me that some also viewed as competition or a threat to their identity or goals. And it was in recognizing that that I began to not only be mindful of my own actions, but especially to my re-actions. Confidence truly is the enemy of competition; whereas, the presence of competition is the lack of confidence. I've never been a competitive woman and absolutely refused to knowingly entertain them. It was always my experience that women see themselves as compared to someone else, who doesn't recognize their own worth and will do almost anything in an effort to prove their self, just as good or better to the point of embracing trifling actions, with that being the only thing proven.

I believe anytime you feel you have to prove yourself to be better than anyone else, it is a result of a void that no amount of despise or disrespect of others or yourself in an attempt to fill will work. Yet, it is the responsibility of those that recognize it to not feed into or respond to it, but to create an opportunity to assist in the discovery and deliverance of it. This can only be done when the individual is ready to scratch the surface and dig deep to address, and uproot the underlying issue and allow replacement with the seed that births purpose. It is said that our greatest challenges are keys to our purpose, and as I look back over my experiences and the path that brought me to where I am, I'd agree. It is essential to understand that no one can help us, if first we are not willing to help ourselves.

It was in accepting, that no matter how much I tried to hide in the background, it wasn't me putting myself out front, but a place that was appointed to me by God, which isn't something you can run or hide from. That made the difference, allowing me to be perfectly comfortable in whom I am and actually being the light. I finally understood that, when you know who you are, it doesn't add to or take away from anyone else, but sincerely encourages others.

"You are not responsible for other people's insecurities; you are only responsible for your response to them. Don't dull yourself down for others to feel better about themselves, that's

54

between them and God. That isn't your job to fix."- Cynthia A.
Patterson - That was a life changing statement by my mentor.
This was a significant statement, because it was honest and
empowering. God will provide you with someone that will as-
sist you in the process of purpose. There were people around
me that separated me from my authenticity. I was putting on a
show and being who I thought people would like or be com-
fortable with; and they still didn't. So I had to rediscover me. It
was during the process, I learned something vitally important
that changed me. I came to the realization that anyone that
wants you to stop being you, because they feel inferior, inse-
cure or "not as good", is based on the way they love or don't
love themselves; and it starts with me loving myself enough to
trust God and being confident in the wisdom from my mentor.

The encouragement I received from the book of Ruth, as well
as my Mentor, is that you are not defined by your past; and it
has no claim on you. "It Had To Happen" to make you BET-
TER. I've heard the saying only the strong survive, and I be-
lieve it is true; because, God knows that we will not only strug-
gle in our testimony, but that we will in fact GET THROUGH!

There are times in our life when the experiences we had at-
tempted to dictate, cripple, distract or deter us from our future.
We have to change our mind and let go of the pain and dis-
appointment we feel toward ourselves and others, in order to

embrace the purpose God has for us.

Sometimes that's the hardest thing to do, because like Orpah, we're stuck; plus, all we can see is our past. All we feel is its pain. In addition, we become more comfortable with the pain and disappointment. It takes courage to love and accept self-flaws and all. The good, the bad, and the ugly, our Beautiful-God sees it all in us; yet He still loves us anyway. The challenge is seeing it in ourselves, accepting it and continuing to become better today than we were yesterday.

In this life, it isn't about competing against someone that will never walk in your shoes, it is solely about knowing who you are, whose you are and loving you unconditionally. Full acceptance is the destination where you discover your purpose. "She said to her, ' all that you say, I will do,' - Ruth 3:5. Having a mentor reestablished my faith in women who help women, gave me accountability, which allowed me to stop hiding from myself, own my mistakes and be committed to my future.

It's Not What People Say About You

Wow! You should be encouraged right now by April; she just said it all in a "nut shell". She gets it. She understands the relationship of Ruth and Naomi as she so illustrated. Likewise, you should encourage your mentee to make the sheer determination to know it is not what people say about you; it is about what you say about yourself. One small positive thought can change her world. God divinely has a plan for her life. He has established promises in His Word that is to personally help her. However, girlfriend, it is so up to you to be driven to move forward and impart every ounce of wisdom you have on the inside of you to make it happen. It is important that she moves forward by taking a stance to know her life matters, and you encouraging her to give herself permission to live in her own personal truth.

Could it be that as her mentor, you have something hidden? Could it be you are hiding behind the title? Well here is a life-changing question for you: How do you have the confidence to know you are capable of helping someone? For many of us, we have taken the bystander approach to our own lives. We allow others to dictate who we are, what we should do, and what we should be doing in life. Our inability to have confidence in whom we are and to stand in our own personal truth is superficial. We lose sight of who we are and will begin to depend on the advice and approval of others, before we can even stop to think for ourselves. The tragedy is that we never give consideration to our own thinking. We just don't trust what we know. We play these thoughts over and over in our mind, and assume others have the direct line to God and not us. At least that is what the enemy wants you to believe.

As a mentor, I learned something vitally important. Something that forever changed me. I share this with many of my mentees. And that is this: no one knows your personal truth. That is between you and God. No one can tell you. Of course, they may try to tell you what the Bible says. They can tell you their opinion; they can give wise counsel. However, no one knows your personal truth like you do. Truth be told, much of the counsel people give is based on their own experience, and you have to definitely measure it to what God says. Am I saying you shouldn't have a mentor that will give you wise counsel? Absolutely not! I am saying there are things that you don't know that maybe others in your life, which you RESPECT and TRUST enormously, may know. That is why I love my mentee April. She is one who stands in her personal truth.

Today may God give your eyes the ability to see the beauty only the heart can understand. If you don't like the situation you are in, you are the only one with the power to change it. Girlfriend, embrace this new you. It looks good! Now walk in your calling; there are women waiting on your help. They are still yoked up, and God has anointed you to be the one to speak life in their situation. So what are you waiting on?

Chapter 7 - Living Life Now!

I found that you cannot take care of others,
if you are always broken.

— Cynthia D.

Cynthia D's Story

*I*have to admit; it has not always been easy for me to say ex-
*actly what is on my mind. I grew up being a people pleaser
and being admonished for having the audacity to speak my
mind. Even when I spoke out against my abuser as a child, I
was silenced. That fire still burns in me to stand up for what I
believe in, speak what is on my mind and to pursue the things
that others say that I cannot have. I decided to step out on faith
and discover who God created me to be. I decided that I have
to live life to the full. I had to find me, Cynthia, while fighting
my way through the voices of what others thought I should do,
should be or should say. It is easy to lose yourself in a society's
idea of what a woman should be. I had become what everyone
else wanted me to be, rather than nurturing who I am.*

*I was dying a slow death. I was catering to the needs of
others, pretending to be someone that I was not. When you*

are being anything but yourself, it is obvious to others. The journey of becoming me was birthed out of years of emotional pain, physical, mental and sexual abuse, overcoming many disappointments and a painful divorce.

I was married twenty-one years and living what most called the "American Dream". My husband was an Ivy League graduate with a six figure salary. We had the house, the children, the cars and the illusion of a blissful life. I played the role, until one day, I discovered that I was living a lie. My husband was living a double life with multiple affairs; but I stayed. For the public, I continued to pretend that everything was good. I was miserable, lonely, but I thought to myself that life has to be better than this. I stayed in the marriage out of fear. I feared what others would think of me, what people would say; because, it was perceived that we had it all. I stayed much too long. It ate away at my soul, all because I was too afraid to live. I believed the lies that had been told to me as a young lady. I had the tapes playing in my head that I was nothing more than a baby making machine and that I would never amount to anything. I was told that if something ever happened to dissolve our marriage, that it would be something that I did. I lived in a prison created in my mind.

I finally got the courage to leave my situation and learn how to live. I began to discover how to live my life to the full. I filed for divorce, which was a difficult decision and process. I returned to college completing and graduated Summa Cum Laude. While in school, I began to discover myself. I learned to like me. What others thought of me became less important. I learned that taking care of me was not being selfish, but was applying self-care. I found that you cannot take care of others, if you are always broken. I learned to live life fully by first taking good care me, and then giving to others in areas that I was passionate about. If there were things that I wanted to do that brought pleasure to my life, I explored it. I made a decision to do whatever I wanted to do within the bounds of God's Word.

I found that living for yourself is vital in becoming all that God has created you to be. I believe that God created us to serve others, but He did not create us to be misused and abused. I was 40 plus years old before I realized the importance of living for me, even while serving others. It was a delicate balance as a parent to live for me, because I had my children's needs to consider. I had to find balance and not over commit myself, especially, to projects that I was not passionate about. I used to put everyone and everything before myself, but not anymore. Since I have made those changes, I am much happier; and, I do not experience as much burnout.

After really examining all that has happened to me in life, I have learned to pay attention to what is happening to me and around me. When I found myself in a healthy and happy place, I learned to recognize things that were not good for me or entrapped me in the past before it becomes a problem. For instance, when life's circumstances became too tough for me, I had a tendency to reach for other people to soothe my broken-ness. I learned to reach for God, and it was very hard in the beginning; but now, I am able to recognize the signs of a prob-lem before they become problems. I also learned the value of saying no, and saying it without explanation.

I have spent almost my entire life trying to please others. Even if it was harmful to me, I would go along with it, because I was taught that you do not rock the boat. I was silenced, even when I had been raped by my own pastor. I think silence is death to your soul, when you have been violated in such a way. I discovered that you must speak up and speak out against vi-olence and sexual abuse. You must speak up when someone purposely mistreats you; because after all, we teach people how to treat us when we are silence or speaking out.

It took me a long time to have confidence in the idea that prayer changes things, because it was always "church folks" who had wounded me, including my ex-husband. People, who should have nurtured me, violated me; but, Cynthia Patterson would always say, "Let's pray". I learned how to stand on God's Word, no matter what. Cynthia allowed me to be real and raw about my feelings about life, my circumstances, my pain, and what others had done to me. Cynthia allowed me to vent, but she always pointed me back to the principles of righteous living and prayer.

As I look back on the past three years of my life, I am amazed at how God has blessed me and opened doors for me. As soon as I took steps of faith, the doors began to open for me. I now give myself permission to live, to feel, to love and to accept that when God created me, He made no mistakes. I learned that you cannot live your life thinking that if only I had this or if only I had that, life would be better. You cannot wait until your circumstances are perfect before you decide to enjoy life. You cannot wait until someone else believes in you. We live in a society where people give up on others easily, so I learned not to be concerned about what others think. I cannot quit, because someone else thinks my thoughts and ideas aren't possible. My favorite scripture is Mark 9:23 where Jesus said everything is possible for one who believes.

The most important lesson I learned in all of my experiences is how to ask the question of what legacy will I leave for my children. Children do not become who you tell them to be; they become who you are. I had to consider if I had remained silent about the sexual abuse in my life and remained in a marriage with a man who was unfaithful, negligent and abusive, what message was I sending to my daughters? More importantly, it wasn't until I discovered my authentic self that I fully understood my value and self-worth. I gained confidence and a positive attitude about life. I discovered that life is about perception. However you perceive a thing to be; it will be.

My best piece of advice for anyone is to be true to you. Realize that you are uniquely created by God. No one else can be you better than you can. You were put here on this planet to do something that no else can do like you can. No matter what you have been through stay with God and be true to you. God has a way of fixing things in such a way that when He is done, you won't look like what you've been through. Important to stay focused, be authentic and stay with God's way of doing things.

We Have to Hold Each Other Accountable

I think much of our power lies in the fact that we are all relational. Talk to any woman; she probably has a number of close friends or she doesn't. Our ability to relate to others and the importance we give to relationships fuels us with the power we need or more importantly it gives us much of our significance. Whether that is right or wrong, I don't know; but, we have to hold each other accountable in fulfilling our ultimate purpose of what God has for us to do on earth. I believe it is God's divine plan and very purpose for us to support one another.

As a mentor, there will be times you will have to go through things. You will have to experience life that will give you a blow that will cause you to want to give up. That will cause you to want to throw in the towel. It's a season where He will test you to see if you are really serious about seeking the things of God. Meaning, God will rewrite the script and have you set your mind on the things above. Why? I believe God is trying to get you to trust Him like never before.

I often say Cynthia is my sister from another mother. We are co-laborers in my organization working with women. The Bible says "iron sharpen iron". You have to understand that you cannot make this alone. You have to have someone who can be there to listen and offer words of encouragement. Leadership is a great task. Being accountable to someone will help you become who God intends for you to be. Being accountable will help you tear down the wall and express how you are feeling. Being accountable is critical to becoming a leader and mentoring others.

Ruth 1:19-21 illustrates this thought that when Naomi and Ruth arrived in Bethlehem:

19 So the two of them continued on their journey. When they came to Bethlehem, the entire town was excited by their arrival. "Is it really Naomi?" the women asked. 20 "Don't call me Naomi," she responded. "Instead, call me Mara, for the

Almighty has made life very bitter for me. 21 I went away full, but the Lord has brought me home empty. Why call me Naomi when the Lord has caused me to suffer and the Almighty has sent such tragedy upon me?"

The name Naomi means "pleasant"; the name Mara means "bitter." Naomi used this to tell the people of Bethlehem that her time away from Israel, her time away from the God of Israel, had not been pleasant—it was bitter. Naomi wasn't a phony. She wasn't going to go home, pretend everything was fine, and be "pleasant". She was going to be honest and say, "Here I am and my life has been bitter." It would have been easy for Naomi to focus on what she had lost. She had lost a husband, two sons, and one daughter-in-law. She had lost all kinds of material possessions. All she had left was one daughter-in-law, Ruth. But through that one thing she had left, God was going to bring unbelievable blessing into her life. God didn't promise days without pain, laughter without sorry, or sun without rain; but, He did promise strength for the day, comfort for the tears, and light for the way. If God bring you to it, He will bring you through it.

No Distractions

Hold your head up. God has no respecter of person. If He did it for Cynthia, He will definitely do it for you. God knows exactly what He is doing in your life. Now He wants you to be encouraged to know who is in control of everything. You have to know that God has not forgotten about you. Although you may have been praying and it appears that nothing has manifested yet, please know He is preparing you for something great. Therefore, today and days to come, stay focused. Don't allow anything to distract you. Take God at His Word and be serious about believing it is all good. You will definitely be blown away by God's power, and you will begin to live your life believing every trial and tribulation eventually reverses; because, your life matters.

Chapter 8 - Celebrating Me

We must live our lives and live on purpose.

— Tamara

Tamara's Story

I have to admit that it has not always been easy for me to be public. I am a very shy and private person. I keep to myself and don't feel comfortable to share personal things that I have gone through in my life, because I don't feel comfortable appearing weak. Psychology labels my personality as introverted. Meaning, I am inclined to be more quiet, reserved and inward-looking. Lately, I have found myself drawn to an organization where I am forced to be in the forefront. I have to push through my discomfort of being such a private person, because my life experiences can help a woman overcome a situation that she may be in. I find it odd that I find myself in these types of groups, but I am not surprised. I have always wanted people to understand that whatever bad experiences they have gone through in life is never an excuse to not move forward.

In my life, several things have happened to me that I had

no control over, and many things have happened because of my bad choices. To name a few things, I have had to endure during my life include being born with a cleft lip and palate which is a birth defect. I had several surgeries from an infant to the age of 17 to attempt to correct the defect. I was made fun of when I was growing up, because I looked different than everyone. Going through life looking different can have a major impact on one's self esteem. I had babies and left home at a young age. I was then in a physically and mentally abusive relationship from the age of 16-20. The abuse was so bad to the point that my family thought I would be in a body bag the next time they saw me. When I finally got out of the relationship, I was stalked and terrorized by my abuser for about six months. I was a single mother with three children struggling day by day raising my kids. I was a woman with a strong desire to meet Mr. Right, get married, and live happily ever after, but there was no Mr. Right in sight. Times in my life were rough, and many times got tougher. One thing after another, these were the things that I was dealing with in my life. I was sick and tired of my life. I felt that life was a big joke and just wasn't fair, but something inside me wouldn't allow life to defeat me. So, I got up every day and put one foot in front of the other and kept moving. I knew that my life had to matter.

At the age of 20, I truly feared for my life and ran from that abusive relationship with my children. In my heart, I believed that he would kill me or severely injure me. I told myself that I would not continue on in that relationship. I got away. I focused on my beautiful children and strived to be the best mother I could be. I paid attention to my children and discovered their strengths and weaknesses. I enrolled them in programs that would help them grow. I made my children my life. Little league football, cheerleading, girl scouts, basketball, and dance classes consumed my life. This went on all throughout elementary school, middle school, and high school.

One day when my older two were in their last years of high school, and my youngest was approaching high school; I realized that I was going to be an empty nester soon. I looked at my life, and though I was very proud of my children and excited about my next chapter, I began to feel lost. I realized at that time that I did not have a life of my own. My world was all about my children. I did not know what my life would look like when they graduated. I began to wonder what in the world would I do with myself. I began to do some deep soul searching and evaluating myself. Who in the heck was I? Why am I here? Am I supposed to be doing anything? These were all questions that I was asking myself, but had no idea of the answers. What I did know was that my life mattered, and I needed be doing something for me. I wasn't particularly religious, but I knew God was doing something with me; He was lining things up for me, sending people in my direction, and ordering

*my footsteps during this transition of my life. I began my jour-
ney to find and discover who I was, and what I was supposed
to be doing in my life in 2007.*

*If you ask most people what is living a full life, they would
probably give you a bucket list of all of the adventurous things
they would like to do before they leave this earth. That is not
the idea that I have in mind, when I think of living a full life.
The word that comes to mind when I think of a full life is wholeness. The idea of living a full life to me means to be healthy
spiritually, mentally, physically, financially, and socially. In
this life, we must live our lives and live on purpose. I did not
have this idea before my journey began. All I knew was I wanted to be financially set and happy, and I was on a mission to
make that happen.*

*The first thing that happened was I was lead to a church,
which was the beginning of my spiritual growth. I was lead
there at the right time. The pastor was preaching sermons
that seemed like they were composed just for me, in which I
was led to join. In that very church, I was connected to Cynthia Patterson, the leader, of the ministry I served. She helped
me so much in my spiritual growth. She's a leader: she listens; she challenges; she ministers with love; and she is now a
friend. She is very supportive, encouraging, and most of all,
she is real. Cynthia has been one of my biggest cheerleaders*

throughout this journey.

My spiritual growth seemed to be the way to improving every area of my life. It helped me mentally and emotionally. The way I thought about things and looked at things began to change. God knew exactly what He was doing. I wanted to grow in every area, so I decided to go back to school. I enrolled in college in 2010, transferred some credits that I had from a local community college in Houston, Texas, graduated and received my degree in 2013. I began working out with a personal trainer in 2010 to make sure that I stayed physically fit. I wanted to be obedient to God's Word and pay my tithes. Honestly, my finances improved when I began tithing. Socially, my life improved after getting involved in church and joining school. I began interacting with people. All facets of my wholeness fell into place, after I focused on my spirituality.

My life began to change, when I started acting like my life mattered. I used to think the statement "You have to take care of yourself before you can take care of others" was such a selfish statement. But now that I have taken the time to focus on me, I now know that this is such a true statement. It is necessary to take care of yourself first. I am a much healthier person inside and out. After taking the time to focus on myself, I can truly help others, because my words don't only come from experience. Now, my words also come from learning and grow-

ing through those experiences.

I know that Cynthia was God sent. She has been a constant these past seven years of my life. She has given me so much wisdom throughout these years. She saw something in me when I first came and joined the ministry she led. I didn't necessarily see anything unique or special about me, but she did. Cynthia and I have had many conversations about any and everything, but for me, it wasn't only about what she said, it was also about how she made me feel when she said it. There is a quote by Dr. Maya Angelou, "I've learned that people will forget what you said, people will forget what you did, but people will never forget how you made them feel." Well that is true when I think about Cynthia. She always makes people feel better after talking to her. She always listens carefully, encourages, and gives you a word. One of the things that I did during my transition is I became a part of DOVE Ministries. My friend, Cynthia Patterson, is the founder and CEO of this organization. Cynthia approached me in 2011 to join her in her ministry. She had been working in her ministry and was about to take it to another level and knew that she would need help from others. She spoke with me about a major role that she thought would be perfect for me. I must admit that I was very shocked. This was a major position, and it was crucial, because it involves people's lives. She believes in me; she is constantly pushing me and encouraging me to step out of my comfort zone, and that speaks volumes.

I believe in people doing the work to improve their life. When I joined DOVE Ministries, all of the leaders were required to go through the developmental training. The training opened my eyes. I learned that I was masking a lot of feelings I was having, and I wasn't really as strong as I alleged to be. Those sessions revealed to me why I behaved in certain manners, and why I allowed myself to go through things that should have immediately made me walk away. The program was yet another door to my journey of finding out who I was, and what I needed to improve. The development training sessions empowered me and gave me true strength. I truly grew in those classes and began to truly understand my purpose and received the necessary tools to help other women. I know that I just didn't make it through, but I have grown through what I have gone through. I believe that that growth will help me help others. When I connect with someone, I like to keep it real. I prefer to have real relationships with people. When I say real relationships, I mean to bond with people. I prefer deep conversation verses small talk. When you have true conversations with people, it allows you to find out who they truly are and vice versa. Several years ago, there was a term people would say, "Keeping it real all the time." I would have close friends or associates that would feel comfortable confiding in me and asking me for my opinion, because they always believed that I would keep it real with them by being honest. I believe in being truthful and honest with people, but never in a hurtful way. My life experience, education, and the tutelage that I received throughout the years gave me the confidence to step out of my comfort zone and help others. I am still an introvert, but I know that there is a time for everything.

Since making the decision to not focus on my circumstances or how unfair I thought life was at times, I chose to look within myself. I chose to learn about myself; and through my journey, I have learned to truly love myself through all of my flaws. Everything that I have endured has made me wiser. I know that God chose me to go through those things, and because of that, I am stronger. I used to look at my achievements or accomplishments as just things that I was supposed to do. I never made a big deal of anything that I did. Now, I look at all of those accomplishments, and I celebrate. Raising three children as a single mother, watching them grow and walk across the stage at their High School graduation and going off to college is an accomplishment, and I celebrate that. I celebrate completing my college education and receiving my Bachelor of Science in Business Management. I celebrate meeting my Mr. Right and my marriage. I celebrate my growth and my transformation. I give myself permission to be happy, to live, to love, and to laugh.

Believe in Yourself

Believing in you is the first secret to success. It helps you to understand the patterns within yourself that is causing inner conflict and pain. You have to respect yourself. It teaches others how you like to be treated. This is very important to have the faith to trust God to be who He has called you to be. Elizabeth Gilbert has been quoted to say, *"Faith is walking face-first and full-speed into the dark. If we truly knew all the answers in advance as to the meaning of life and the nature of God and the destiny of our souls, our belief would not be a leap of faith, and it would not be a courageous act of humanity; it would just be... a prudent insurance policy."*

This quote would fit so well in the character of Naomi. She did not allow her circumstance to change who she was. She stayed true to who she was in God. Ruth 1:16 *And your God, [will be] my God* meant that Naomi's relationship with God made an impact on Ruth. This is striking, because Naomi did not have an easy life. She had been widowed, had lost both her sons, and believed that she had caused each calamity by her disobedience. Yet, she still honored and loved the LORD.

As a mentor/leader, women should be able to look at your life, just as Ruth looked at Naomi's and say, "I want your God to be my God." Your trust in God, and turning towards Him in tough times, will often be the thing that draws others to the LORD. Here is another point in the scripture: "*Your God will be my God*". Look at this, for ten years of Naomi's compromise in Moab never made Ruth confess her allegiance to the God of Israel. Yet, as soon as Naomi stood and said, "I'm going back to the God of Israel, I'll put my fate in His hands," Ruth stood with her. This speaks great volume for you to have as a leader/mentor—Integrity.

This is what I loved about my partner in ministry, Tamara. She did not allow the odds of others' opinion to change her journey to pursuing and seeking God. It was a search that was filled with ups and downs, but she did not allow it to deter her from the promises of God.

Invest in Yourself

I would like to encourage you to love and constantly invest in yourself. We can get so wrapped up in being there for others, that we put ourselves on the back burner. I encourage you to be the best you can be. I encourage you to empower other women. Remember, we are all uniquely made, and you are not in competition with anyone, but yourself. I encourage you to take your life to a higher level. I encourage you to become whole.

Closing

In the introduction, I invited you to join us for dinner and meet your new sister-friends for a girl talk conversation. I could imagine for some of the women, the idea of sharing personal information, would be a very discomfort as shared by Tamara: *"I have to push through my discomfort of being such a private person, because my life experiences can help a woman overcome a situation that she may be in."* In many of the stories you have read, these women had to experience taking off their mask and revealing their true self. Exposing the true you can be a frightening experience. A lot of what the issues were with these women was described as fear, and it is like trying to win a battle without a full army. We need those strengths that God has given each of us, but so often, our strengths also become our weakness and our shame.

Authenticity Sets Up Healthy Boundaries

Though we say, we want authentic relationships, they can be frightening. We judge each other so quickly, and we cut each other down in our judgments. Yet, we need each other just the same, and we need that authenticity painful or not. At least I do, and that is how I mentor other women. Early on in my ministry, what I have found was this: If I am not honest with myself and if I am not willing to look deep within at that darkness, then it stays there. If I cannot go toe to toe with where I am weak, then I am not truthful at all as to whom I am: I am a fake person; I make many excuses; I dare to blame others— it's always someone else's fault. Consequently, I would find myself going to God with the same attitude. I would stand before God with defenses. Sounds familiar? So, how in the world would I expect to help someone else, if I can't be true to myself?

Now that I have matured, there's a hard conviction and accountability I have placed upon myself, and I pray that you also adopt. Make sure that being authentic with the women you mentor is priority. You and I need those authentic relationships in order to live what we have learned with integrity. To live what you have survived often requires bravery, and we need each other to uphold that courage. Our mentees have everything they need inside of them; they just need us to help them pull it out.

You Must Have Active Listening

I believe there are some women that need authentic relationships in their lives to create space. Their fears, their shame and their disappointments end up taking so much space within them. It takes a lot for a woman to open up to another woman—it's called openness. I am sure it was very awkward for the women I initially meet to let me in their space. Nonetheless, I believe God allowed us to endure our relationship through the fruitfulness of the mentorship. I had to learn the art of active listening. It is very important to have this skill when dealing with your mentees. You cannot do all the talking. You have to be able to allow her to share, so she can feel comfortable with you. She needs to know she is not alone, and you understand. Active listening helps you with your discernment. It is the most effective way of breaking through her feelings of isolation and misunderstanding.

Here are a few mistakes we make as mentors when listening to our mentees: 1). Listening as if you ran into her at Walmart. The two of you have a conversation, and you anticipate what you are going to say, as soon as she conveys her story. You are so quick to give her your story. As a result, you take over the conversation. So, I would expect she would wonder did you really hear her; 2). The conversation is not for you to listen and interpret flaws in her thinking with the intent of "straightening her out". Now you have taken on the position as being the conversation police, giving her a ticket for violation of her feelings and thoughts; 3). You don't focus on how she will respond or policing her thought process. Rather, the focus should be to truly understand what she is feeling and thinking. Listen for facts, but more importantly, listen for feelings and thoughts behind the facts. Give attention to all communication, verbal and nonverbal. Subsequently, you can reflect on what she has declared to you.

Empathize With Your Mentee

I found that having empathy for my mentees lets them know their feelings matter. Expressing empathy is so important. Merriam Webster defines "empathy" *as the feeling that you understand and share another person's experiences and emotions: the ability to share someone else's feelings* (Merriam-Webster. com, 2015). In other words, it is putting yourself in her shoes, you see yourself experience what she is sharing with you. This is a very essential prerequisite in order to effectively respond with understanding. However, you must first be in touch with your own feelings, healed, and delivered; so, you won't make the mistake of bringing in "your stuff". Remember I talked about "your stuff" meaning your issues from the past. Thus, I have developed the following characteristics to being Empathetic:

1. Enables you to enter into her world

2. Enables you to enter into her feelings

3. Gives her an understanding

4. Gives her acceptance in her issues

5. Allows you to have a response to her by saying, "That really hurt me."

6. Allows you to have a response by saying, "I am so sorry" or "I am so sorry that happened to you."

7. Allows you to have a response by saying, "I love you" or "I care about you."

Scriptures that come to mind are *James 1:19, "Everyone should be quick to listen, slow to speak."* In case you missed my point, here's a more direct scripture, *"It's stupid and embarrassing to give an answer before you listen." (Proverbs 19:13 CEV)*

Your Mentee Needs To Feel There is Hope

There is one more idea I would like to share that is very important when listening to your mentees and that is being able to be a sounding board, reflect and acquire an understanding. Your mentee has to be able to think through her issue and be able to determine what she should do. In the same way, it is like you holding a mirror in front of her; and it reflects back the image to what she looks like. Likewise, it is what you are doing with her issue. You are helping her to reflect what she is thinking and feeling.

As a mentor, being able to reflect is important. I have found that this process is either painful or fearful. So, early on due to lack of knowledge, my mentees would avoid insensitive answers or direct advice. Hence, as I matured as a mentor, I discovered asking questions that would walk my mentees through a process of decision making. This questioning process used skills that would lessen unhealthy dependency on me, but instead, strengthen her ability to cope with future emotional pain. When I am speaking with my mentees, I ask open-ended questions similar to the following:

1. What are you going to do?

2. What are your options?

3. What roadblocks do you anticipate? How will you move through them?

4. What resources will you need? Where will your support come from?

5. How will the choices you are making now bring you hope?

6. What do you think God wants you to do?

7. Where do you feel God in all of this?

Did you notice that none of these questions required a yes or no answer? All of these questions placed a presenting problem on her shoulder, not yours. It is not your task to figure out what your mentee should do, but it is your role as a mentor to coach her to a viable response or decision. Look at the open-ended question Naomi asked Ruth and Oprah in Ruth 1:12-13. *12 And even if it were possible, and I were to get married tonight and bear sons, then what? 13 Would you wait for them to grow up and refuse to marry someone else?* This question was asked at the right time. It was a moment that allowed transformation to move forward or remain the same. Orpah returned back to Moab, and Ruth decided to stay with Naomi and go to Bethlehem. Likewise, your purpose is to compel transformation as well. You may discuss your own experience in this case to allow further insight in formulating good questions to ask. As a result, this will give your mentee hope by simply reflecting her thinking process through strategic open-ended questions.

Respect The Choices She Make to Move Forward

I had to learn that admiration acknowledges that both of you should be treated with respect and dignity. What I loved about the relationship of Ruth and Naomi is that they respected each other. It was so evident throughout the book of Ruth. As a mentor, respect indicates that your mentee has the ability to feel and make choices differently than you. She has the ability

85

to change herself with help from God. She is responsible for "her stuff", not you. Remember, you are not her savior; God is her savior. There are limits to what you can do for her. You cannot embrace salvation through Jesus Christ for her. You cannot choose faith or morality for her. Please, don't forget this! It will save you so much frustration, doubt and burnout. Respect helps you to establish healthy boundaries. Remember, your mentee wants to be heard, understood, and invited to know God in the midst of her chaos and confusion. Yes, Lord! Let's recap. I cannot stress enough, active listening is very important. It is your responsibility as a mentor to attract your mentees—even with issues and drama—to the heart of God through empathy, reflection, and respectful listening.

Knowing Your Place As A Mentor

I am so proud of each of these brave women that have shared. They have broken learned false beliefs or myths. They have stepped up. They have put themselves out here; and now, it is safe for you to do so too. As I listened to story after story of these remarkable women, I saw many threads that wove us all together. As I noted earlier, one of them was fear. Everyone was afraid of something. To be real with you, to be real with others is actually pretty frightening. It certainly opens you up for judgment, for criticism, and to set you up for the lie the enemy has told you. However, God wants you to know the truth.

Through all of the experiences, I have learned from each of the women is "what I can do and "what I cannot do" in mentoring other women. And through this draining experience, I developed these guidelines for mentoring.

What I can do	*What I cannot do*
1. Be a listener	*1. Change her*
2. Designate time to be available	*2. Go without regular sleep*
3. Get more help	*3. Do it all alone.*
4. Pray for her	*4. Cure her hurts or fix it*
5. Suggest professional help for her	*5. Erase her past pain/ choices*

I have adopted this list from mentors that mentored me and discovery from the women I am mentoring. This is a list that had to be established and forced me to set healthy boundaries and realistic expectations. Unlimited listening time and twenty-four/seven availability, alone, are not the solution for another woman's problems. Checking the list when I felt the urge to fix her problems would have confirmed my decision to do only "What I can do" while acknowledging "What I cannot do". (Hislop, 2003)

The right decision positions you for Favor with God. Ruth 2:10-12 is so profound *"At this, she bowed down with her face to the ground. She exclaimed, "Why have I found such favor in your eyes that you notice me—a foreigner?"* [11] *Boaz replied, "I've been told all about what you have done for your moth-er-in-law since the death of your husband—how you left your father and mother and your homeland and came to live with a people you did not know before.* [12] *May the LORD repay you for what you have done. May you be richly rewarded by the LORD, the God of Israel, under whose wings you have come to take refuge."* ~ *(New Living Translation)*

Wow, these scriptures are something to really shout to the roof top and jump for joy, because there is a lesson to be learned from this moment. When we begin to develop our spiritual selves without neglecting ourselves, exciting things happen. God used Ruth to get her into the place that He needed in order to fulfill His plan. He used Naomi in the same way for His glory. The Holy Spirit draws women to us, so they can come to know the Savior, who makes our lives shine and our hearts overflow with joy and love.

Don't get me wrong. We should never waste time in fulfill-ing the purpose that God has for us to help women. We also don't want to waste God's time on superfluous matters. I'm sure you don't either. Now there will be times, however, when we may get bogged down with life issues. We will not be able to take the time we need to be our best. We will not be able to take care of ourselves or spend time with God. We will stop believing that there is anything better for us, than what we are experiencing right now. That will be far from the truth! It is a lie from the enemy.

Always remember you are on a journey with your mentee. God will direct you to guide her through the Holy Spirit and through His word. You always want to be a support to your mentee in every way. I know you can do it. Here is a word of caution. Please don't keep putting your life on hold waiting to arrive at the destination (in this case, your purpose).

You may have said, "God, you want to use me?" Or, "I don't think I am worthy for this," or, "I've made a lot of mistakes," or "How can I give someone advice, when I don't have it all together." Just like Ruth, God has noticed you. He has heard every prayer that you prayed. In spite of all you have gone through, your willingness to pursue God and not quit has positioned you in God's favor. He is moving you to another place in Him. You are probably asking what I mean another place. I discovered the distance between Moab and Bethlehem was an upward movement. In other words, God is trying to take you higher as a mentor. I believe God is using me to help with your positioning. It's a blessing for mentors to openly share their experiences. Nevertheless, God expects you to be obedient to His word and resources in order to take you higher. In Hebrew, Bethlehem means "house of bread". In other words, God wants to bless you with a mentee, so you can help her reach the full potential He has predestined for her.

In the following pages, I have provided you scriptures to pray: prayers of repentance, refocus, and reposition yourself into the place God has called you. I have just shared with you in transparency my journey as a mentor. Am I done? Absolutely not! There is so much more I am learning. Here's my question to you: Are you willing to be a part of God's provision in the lives of women like the ones that shared their story in this book? Remember, "Your Life Matters" and the women you help Life Matters Too!

PRAYER SCRIPTURES OF REPENTANCE

Psalm 51:10

Create in me a clean heart, O God. Renew a loyal spirit within me.

Psalm 32:5

Finally, I confessed all my sins to you and stopped trying to hide my guilt. I said to myself, "I will confess my rebellion to the Lord." And you forgave me! All my guilt is gone.

Psalm 24:10

Who is the King of glory? The Lord of Heaven's Armies— he is the King of glory.

Job 34:32

For 'I don't know what evil I have done, tell me. If I have done wrong, I will stop at once'?

Psalm 42:8

But each day the Lord pours his unfailing love upon me, and through each night I sing his songs, praying to God who gives me life.

Psalm 19:12-14

How can I know all the sins lurking in my heart? Cleanse me from these hidden faults.

13 Keep your servant from deliberate sins! Don't let them control me.

Then I will be free of guilt and innocent of great sin.

Psalm 32:5

Finally, I confessed all my sins to you and stopped trying to hide my guilt. I said to myself, "I will confess my rebellion to the Lord." And you forgave me! All my guilt is gone.

PRAYER SCRIPTURES TO HELP YOU REFOCUS

Job 42:1-6 (Message Bible)

"I'm convinced: You can do anything and everything. Nothing and no one can upset your plans. You asked, 'Who is this muddying the water, ignorantly confusing the issue, second-guessing my purposes?' I admit it. I was the one. I babbled on about things far beyond me, made small talk about wonders way over my head. You told me, 'Listen, and let me do the talking. Let me ask the questions. You give the answers. 'I admit I once lived by rumors of you; now I have it all firsthand—from my own eyes and ears! I'm sorry—forgive me. I'll never do that again, I promise! I'll never again live on crusts of hearsay, crumbs of rumor."

Philippians 3:13-14

13 No, dear brothers and sisters, I have not achieved it,[a] but I focus on this one thing: Forgetting the past and looking forward to what lies ahead, 14 I press on to reach the end of the race and receive the heavenly prize for which God, through Christ Jesus, is calling us.

Psalm 66:19-20

19 But God did listen! He paid attention to my prayer. 20 Praise God, who did not ignore my prayer or withdraw his unfailing love from me.

Psalm 62:5-7, 9 (Message Bible)

5-6 God, the one and only— I'll wait as long as he says. Everything I hope for comes from him, so why not? He's a solid rock under my feet, breathing room for my soul, An impregnable castle: I'm set for life. 7-9 My help and glory are in God —granite-strength and safe-harbor-God— Man as such is smoke, woman as such, a mirage. Put them together, they're nothing; two times nothing is nothing.

Exodus 15:2

The Lord is my strength and my song; he has given me victory. This is my God, and I will praise him— my father's God, and I will exalt him!

Psalm 119:23

Even princes sit and speak against me, but I will meditate on your decrees.

2 Tim 4:17

But the Lord stood with me and gave me strength so that I might preach the Good News in its entirety for all the Gentiles to hear. And he rescued me from certain death

Psalm 121:1-2

1 I look up to the mountains— does my help come from there? 2 My help comes from the Lord, who made heaven and earth!

PRAYER SCRIPTURES TO HELP YOU REPOSITION

Psalm 26:2

Now I stand on solid ground, and I will publicly praise the Lord.

Exodus 33:13

If it is true that you look favorably on me, let me know your ways so I may understand you more fully and continue to enjoy your favor. And remember that this nation is your very own people."

Psalm 86:11

Teach me your ways, O Lord, that I may live according to your truth! Grant me purity of heart, so that I may honor you.

Psalm 143:8-10

Let me hear of your unfailing love each morning, for I am trusting in you. Show me where to walk, for I give myself to you. 9 Rescue me from my enemies, Lord; I run to you to hide me. 10 Teach me to do your will, for you are my God. May your gracious Spirit lead me forward on a firm footing.

Psalm 73:24

You guide me with your counsel, leading me to a glorious destiny.

Psalm 25:4-5

4 Show me the right path, O Lord; point out the road for me to follow. 5 Lead me by your truth and teach me, for you are the God who saves me. All day long I put my hope in you.

Notes

1. Cherry, K. (2014). *Stages of Change*. Retrieved from Psychology.about.com: http://psychology.about.com/od/behavioralpsychology/ss/behaviorchange_8.htm

2. Elizabeth Gilbert, *"Faith is walking face-first and full-speed into the dark. If we truly knew all the answers in advance as to the meaning of life and the nature of God and the destiny of our souls, our belief would not be a leap of faith, and it would not be a courageous act of humanity; it would just be... a prudent insurance policy."*

3. Evans, R. P. (2008) "Grace: A Novel". New York: Simon & Schuster

4. Hislop, B. (2003). The Skill of Shrperding Women. In B. W. Hislop, *Shepherding: A Woman's Heart* (p. 137). Chicago: Moody Publishers.

5. Jack Frost, *"what reveals a genuine love for God is my ability to convince my family and others of my love for them."*

6. Martin Luther King, Jr., *"Take the first step in faith. You don't have to see the whole staircase, just take the first step."*

7. *Merriam-Webster.com*. (2015, January 9). Retrieved January 9, 2015, from Merriam-Webster: http://www.merriam-webster.com/dictionary/empathy

8. Patterson, C.A. (2011) *"It Had to Happen: Understanding Everything You Go Through in Life is for God's Purpose"*. Texas: Heavenly Realm Publishing

9. Zig Zigler, *"You cannot consistently perform in a manner which is inconsistent with the way you see yourself"*.

Suggestions for women who choose to form an accountability group out of this book.

1. Accountability partners are keys in your life in becoming better.

2. Come to the group prepared and prayed up. You will find that careful preparation will greatly enrich your time spent in group discussion.

3. Be willing to participate in the discussion. Encouraging each other in the group to discuss what you discovered about yourself. Always stick to the topic being discussed.

4. Be sensitive to the others in the group. Listen attentively to each other's testimony. You may be surprised by their insights!

5. Remember that anything said in the group is confidential and should not be discussed outside of your group, unless specific permission is given to do so.

About the Author

Cynthia A. Patterson is a native Houstonian. She is an anointed woman of God, specializing in spiritual growth development and empowerment. Cynthia shares with many her testimony where she lived a double life, working in Corporate America by day then drugs, alcohol, and the adult entertainment industry by night. While this lifestyle was very gratifying, it turned out, she chose to live this way to suppress the feelings of guilt, shame, abandonment, and humiliation, that she acquired from her entire negative past experiences through violent domestic and sexual abuse. So for years, she was pursuing something that only fixed those issues temporarily, by satisfying a desire for a momentary high or rush. Lost with no hope, this left her feeling dead on the inside. Cynthia recognized and sought a higher power for her help and strength. Now her mission in life is committed to helping women identify their significant purpose in life.

A sought-after inspirational speaker, who has a genuine passion to inspire and encourage women, she is known for her amazing, approachable, engaging, and transparent style. Her deep love for God is obvious, as she takes her audience on a journey through the truth of God's word, in all her presentations. Her wisdom is shared with loads of practical advice and application. No matter what the topic, her passion and prayer is that every woman or teenage girl duplicates the message and be inspired.

Contact Information

Join Cynthia in her movement to minister the Gospel of Jesus Christ to women of all walks of life. She speaks on topics such as:

This Girl is on Fire!

What's Your Problem?

When it doesn't get better, but worse

Don't Give up!

Becoming a Woman of Wisdom

Living Your Best Life!

Single for a Season

...and so much more!

If you wish for Cynthia to come and speak at your women's conferences, workshops, seminars, women retreats, or group coaching, please request via email at info@dove-ministries. org. Please visit her ministry website at www.dove-ministries. org for other product and services. Stay connected with Cynthia through social media:

Twitter: cyndypatterson
Facebook: Cynthiapatterson
Instagram: cynthiapatterson

It Had to Happen

Understanding that Everything You Go Through in Life is for God's Purpose

It Had to Happen is an inspiring book that will heal wounds, restore your faith and dramatically change your relationship with God. After carefully retracing your steps, you will be able to identify with the direction you are heading and begin your journey with confidence and faith. During this process, you'll learn:

- The secrets needed to pursue your purpose.

- To enjoy the success of finding out who you really are.

And most importantly, understand that past mistakes simply, HAD TO HAPPEN!

It Had to Happen is available on Amazon, Barnes & Noble and other online book stores.

Live **BETTER** Everyday

Believing Every Trial and Tribulation Eventually Reverses

Cynthia A. Patterson

A 4-Week Prayer Journey to Inspire You to Live Better

Live *BETTER* Everyday

Believing Every Trial and Tribulation Eventually Reverses

Are you sick and tired of being sick and tired? Do you feel like your life is stuck? Are you held back by past challenges or pain?

Live Better Everyday will inspire you to let your dreams rise to new heights as a world of possibilities waits to be discovered. Be inspired and encouraged through prayers, reflections, and affirmations to better your hopes and plans for the future.

Wherever you may have been and whatever you may have done, you will Live BETTER Everyday!

* 9 7 8 0 6 9 2 3 6 3 3 9 3 *